The Plant Book

Dr Brian Knapp and Peter Riley

Atlantic Europe Publishing

First published in 2001 by
Atlantic Europe Publishing Company Ltd.

Copyright © 2001
Atlantic Europe Publishing Company Ltd.

Authors
Dr Brian Knapp, BSc, PhD, and Peter Riley, BSc

Art Director
Duncan McCrae, BSc

Senior Designer
Adele Humphries, BA, PGCE

Editors
Lisa Magloff, BA, and Barbara Bass, BA

Designed and produced by
EARTHSCAPE EDITIONS

Reproduced in Malaysia by
Global Colour

Printed in Hong Kong by
Wing King Tong Company Ltd.

Suggested cataloguing location
Knapp, Brian and Riley, Peter
The Plant Book – *Curriculum Visions*
    1. Plants
    I. Title II. Series
581

Paperback ISBN 1 86214 078 2
Hardback ISBN 1 86214 088 X

Illustrations
All illustrations by *David Woodroffe*

Picture credits
All photographs are from the Earthscape
Editions photolibrary.

Curriculum Visions

Curriculum Visions is a registered trademark of
Atlantic Europe Publishing Company Ltd.

Glossary
There is a glossary on pages 46-47.
Glossary terms are referred to in the
text by using CAPITALS.

Index
There is an index on page 48.

Teacher's Guide
There is a Teacher's Guide to
accompany this book, available
only from this publisher.

Dedicated Web Site
There's more about other great
Curriculum Visions packs and a wealth
of supporting information available at
our dedicated web site. Visit:

www.CurriculumVisions.com

Cactus with spines as defence

Pond weeds giving out oxygen

Contents

A rainforest tree with buttress roots

Plants

Plants grow nearly everywhere in the world, both on land and in the sea. The place where a plant lives and grows is called its HABITAT. Because conditions vary so widely over the world, there are many habitats and many kinds of plants.

① A plant uses its **ROOT** to hold it in the ground and take in water and **MINERALS**. Some roots have other uses too. These are shown on pages 6–7.

② The **SHOOT** is all of the plant above ground. It is made of a **STEM**, which supports the **LEAVES** and **FLOWERS**, and carries food and water to all parts of the plant. Find out how the stem works on pages 8–9.

③ Leaves soak up sunlight and make food for the plant. There are many kinds of leaves, as you can see on pages 10–11.

④ Leaves are made from tiny building blocks called **CELLS**. There are different kinds of cells in a plant. Groups of cells make new materials called **TISSUES**. Find out more about cells on pages 12–13.

⑤ Plants use sunlight as **ENERGY** for growing new tissue. See what else plants need in order to grow on pages 14–15.

⑥ The flower is the colourful or scented part of the plant that attracts **INSECTS**, birds and bats.

The parts of the flower that do this are described on pages 16–17.

⑦ Plants produce **SEEDS** when **POLLEN** grains are carried from the flowers of one plant to another. The two types of **POLLINATION** are shown on pages 18–19.

⑧ Many plants do not have flowers. Some, like **CONIFERS**, still have pollen, while others produce **SPORES**. Find out about these on page 21.

⑨ There are many ways in which seeds are scattered far from their parent plant. Find out how this happens on pages 22–23.

⑩ Seeds sprout in a process called **GERMINATION**. Find out what conditions the seeds need for germination on pages 24–25.

⑪ Some plants do not need seeds at all. They can grow new plants from their stems. Find out how on pages 26–27.

⑫ Plants use **SPINES**, **THORNS** and **POISONS** for defence. Find out other ways plants defend themselves on pages 28–29.

⓭ Some plants grow very fast and live for just one season. These are the **ANNUALS**. See how this helps them compete on pages 30–31.

⓮ Plants called **PERENNIALS** grow year after year. They are often the largest plants in an area, as you can see on pages 32–33.

⓯ Different parts of the world have different kinds of weather and so different types of plants. You can see these many **HABITATS** on pages 34–35.

⓰ A **WOODLAND** is an example of a habitat which changes dramatically throughout the year. Find out how this affects the plants that grow there on pages 36–37.

⓱ Many different types of plant grow in and around water. Find out more about them on pages 38–39.

⓲ Find out how plants survive the cold of mountain winters on pages 40–41.

⓳ Giant **EVERGREEN** trees grow in the **TROPICAL RAINFOREST**. You can see how they grow on pages 42–43.

⓴ Deserts are difficult places for plants to grow and many **ADAPT** in special ways. Some of these are shown on pages 44–45.

Roots

The ROOT is like an anchor, holding the plant in the ground. Roots also take in water and nourishment and may also store food.

The root is what holds the plant into the **SOIL**. Some plants have a thick central root called the **TAP ROOT**. It grows downwards through the soil. Side roots grow outwards from the tap root (picture ①). Other plants have thin roots all of a similar size. These are called **FIBROUS ROOTS** (picture ②).

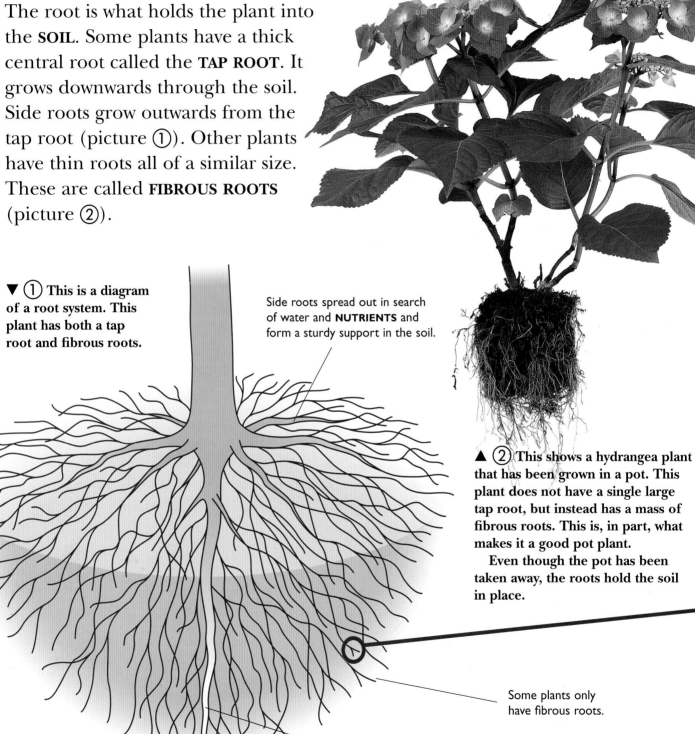

▼ ① This is a diagram of a root system. This plant has both a tap root and fibrous roots.

Side roots spread out in search of water and **NUTRIENTS** and form a sturdy support in the soil.

▲ ② This shows a hydrangea plant that has been grown in a pot. This plant does not have a single large tap root, but instead has a mass of fibrous roots. This is, in part, what makes it a good pot plant.
  Even though the pot has been taken away, the roots hold the soil in place.

Some plants only have fibrous roots.

The tap root burrows down into the soil to anchor the plant and to find water during drought.

The ends of the roots are covered in root hairs (picture ③).

Taking up water and nourishment

Plants need nourishment. Most of the food a growing plant needs is dissolved in water in the soil. Some of this is sucked into the plant through its roots.

Storing water and food

Some plants also use their roots to store food and water. To do this the root must swell up. Usually, it is the tap root that swells (picture ④).

▶ ④ **The carrot plant has an enlarged tap root and almost no fibrous roots.**

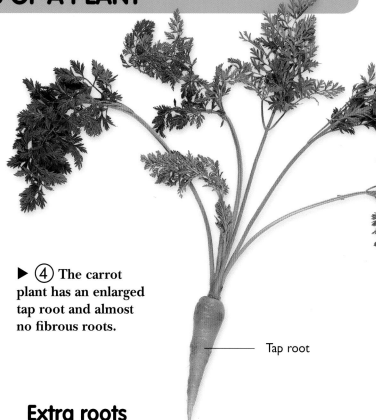

Tap root

▼ ③ **This is the end of a root. It is covered in hairs. Root hairs are so small they are difficult to see without a microscope.**

Water and **MINERALS** pass through the root hairs into larger passageways to reach other parts of the plant where they are needed for nourishment.

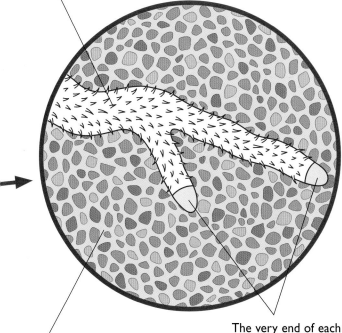

Water between soil particles contains dissolved minerals. The minerals are the nourishment the plant needs.

The very end of each root has a tough skin which protects it as it burrows its way through the soil.

Extra roots

Roots will form on many parts of a plant. Some plants can even grow roots all along their stems (picture ⑤).

Gardeners use this property when making cuttings. When such a cutting is taken and placed into moist soil, it will grow new roots. Some **LEAVES** can also be placed on damp soil and they too will grow new roots.

▲ ⑤ **Ivy can cling on to trees and brick walls using extra roots that grow all along its stem.**

Stems

The STEM rises from the roots. It carries water from the roots to the leaves and flowers, and food to all parts of the SHOOT.

The stem is like a large, flexible post, holding the plant upright. The stem carries food and water from the roots to the leaves and the flowers.

Stems hold a plant upright

There are two kinds of stem. Small plants, like grasses, have light, flexible, soft stems, often called **STALKS** (picture ①). These stems are held upright by **FIBRES**. These fibres are what make stems 'stringy' to eat. The fibres are very strong and do not break easily.

◀ ① Stalks support leaves and flowers. The stalks carry water and food up and down the plant, and allow the leaves to rise up and spread out to get more sunlight.

▲ ③ Giant redwoods are the world's largest trees. Their stems can be 100m tall, 6m across and can weigh 6000 tonnes.

▼ ② The centre of a tree trunk is made of solid wood; only the outside is alive. The outside grows and adds a new layer each year, called TREE RINGS.

The surface is covered by a protective 'skin' of **BARK**.

The outer ring is the 'live' and growing part of the tree adding a new layer each year.

Tree rings show changes in growth through the seasons – fast growth (light coloured) in spring and slower growth (dark coloured) in the summer. There is no growth in the winter.

The dead wood in the centre hardens, making the stem stronger.

The stalks are also held up by the water inside them and easily bend over (wilt) when the soil dries out.

Other kinds of stems are woody. They are often called **TRUNKS**. Their centres are made of strong wood (pictures ② and ③). They are still slightly flexible, but they do not wilt in times of drought.

Stems transfer water and food

All stems contain a network of tiny tubes that carry food and water around the plant.

There are two sets of tubes, one for food, the other for water. The food tubes carry food, that has been made in the leaves, down to the roots and up to the flowers. The water tubes carry water upwards from the roots to the leaves and flowers (pictures ④ and ⑤).

In small plants the food and water tubes are grouped together. In large woody plants, the tubes are arranged in a ring around the outside of the stem.

Stems can store food and water

Stems can be used to store both food and water. A **CACTUS** does this by growing a stem that can swell up.

Close-up of a cross section through one of the celery stems

▲ ④ You can follow the way water moves in a plant by placing sticks of celery in a jar of dyed water. Over a few hours, you can see the coloured water rise in the stalks, as it makes its way up the water-carrying tubes near the outside of the stem.

▶ ⑤ The water and food-carrying tubes are the small holes between the ribs of this stem. This stem belongs to a vine.

9

Leaves

Leaves are thin blades which soak up sunlight and make food for the plant.

A plant is mainly made up of leaves. Leaves are usually flat, wide blades, like sails. Their job is to spread out and catch as much sunlight as possible, and in this way make food for the growing plant (pictures ① and ②).

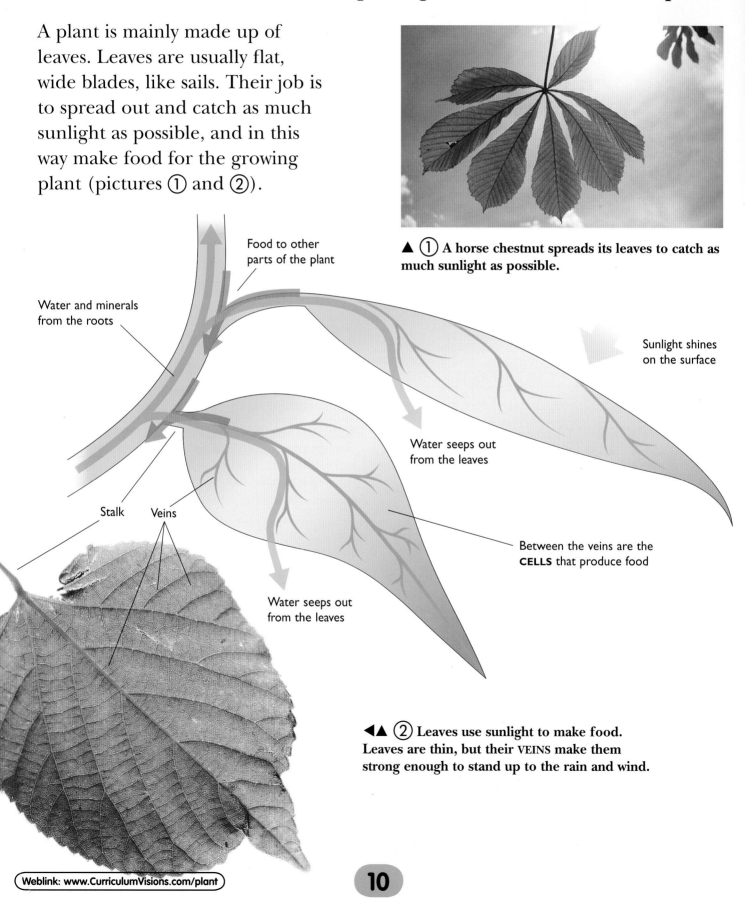

▲ ① A horse chestnut spreads its leaves to catch as much sunlight as possible.

Food to other parts of the plant

Water and minerals from the roots

Sunlight shines on the surface

Water seeps out from the leaves

Stalk   Veins

Between the veins are the **CELLS** that produce food

Water seeps out from the leaves

◄▲ ② Leaves use sunlight to make food. Leaves are thin, but their VEINS make them strong enough to stand up to the rain and wind.

Each leaf has a stalk, from which branches a network of **VEINS**. The veins provide the support for the leaf and also carry food and water between the leaf and other parts of the plant.

The stalk and the veins are made of a tough material, whereas the bulk of the leaf – called the **BLADE** – is softer.

Most flowering trees have broad leaves, which is why they are called **BROADLEAVED TREES. CONIFERS** (pine trees etc.), and many other plants that keep their leaves during winter or over a long dry season, often have long, thin leaves called **NEEDLES** (picture ③).

Leaf patterns

If you look at the leaves on a plant, you will see that they are arranged in patterns (picture ④). This is so all the leaves can receive as much light as possible, to make food.

Some leaves are arranged alternately, others are in pairs, while yet others are in a whorl or a rosette pattern.

▼ ③ **Needles on most conifer trees are tough and stand up to snow, wind and cold.**

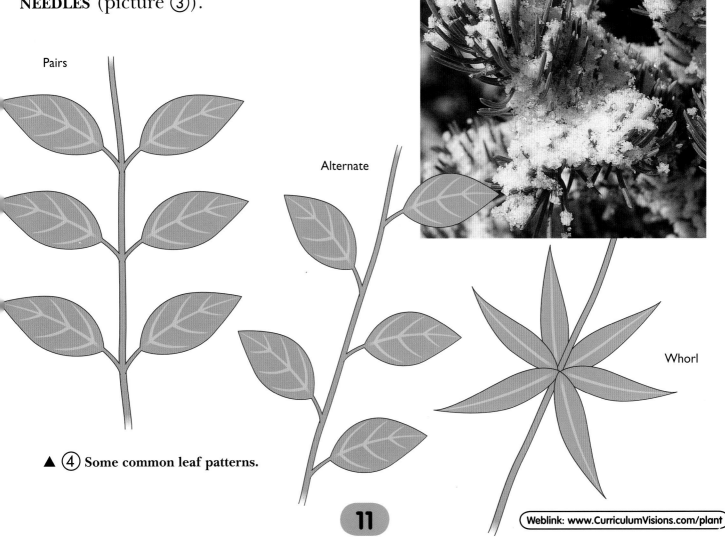

Pairs

Alternate

Whorl

▲ ④ **Some common leaf patterns.**

Weblink: www.CurriculumVisions.com/plant

Inside a leaf

Leaves are made of several layers. Each layer has a special part to play.

In order to make food, a plant needs light, water and dissolved minerals from the ground, and a supply of air.

All of these things are turned into food in the leaves.

But the leaf also has to stand up to the battering of the wind and the rain. For this reason every leaf has several layers.

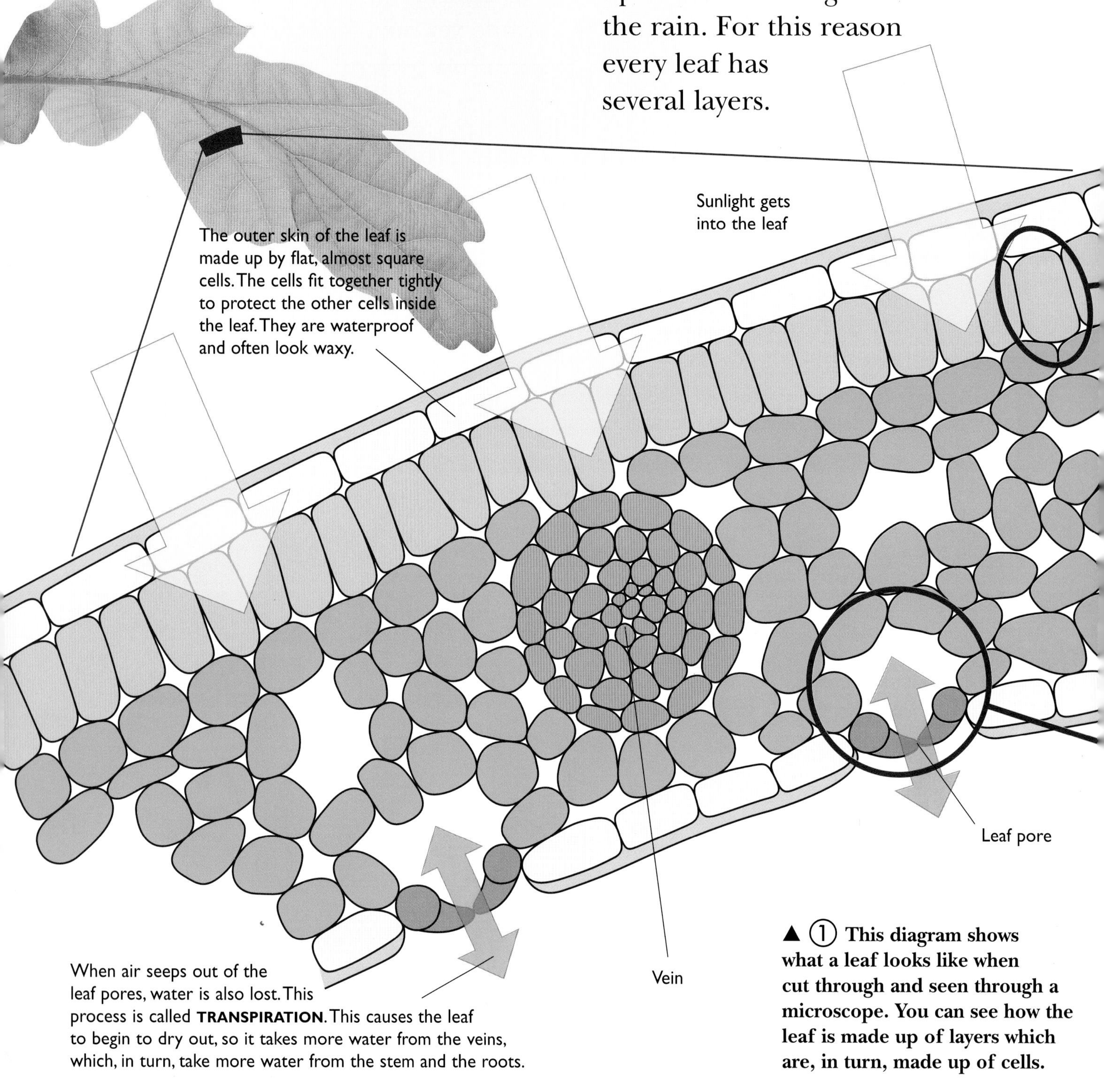

Sunlight gets into the leaf

The outer skin of the leaf is made up by flat, almost square cells. The cells fit together tightly to protect the other cells inside the leaf. They are waterproof and often look waxy.

Leaf pore

When air seeps out of the leaf pores, water is also lost. This process is called **TRANSPIRATION**. This causes the leaf to begin to dry out, so it takes more water from the veins, which, in turn, take more water from the stem and the roots.

Vein

▲ ① This diagram shows what a leaf looks like when cut through and seen through a microscope. You can see how the leaf is made up of layers which are, in turn, made up of cells.

Leaf cells

Each layer of a leaf is made of tiny bags of material called **CELLS**.

Groups of cells of the same type often join together. Cells are so small that you need a microscope to see them (picture ①).

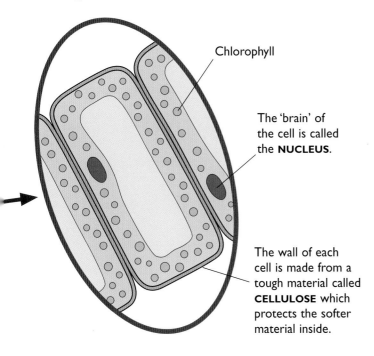

Chlorophyll

The 'brain' of the cell is called the **NUCLEUS**.

The wall of each cell is made from a tough material called **CELLULOSE** which protects the softer material inside.

Most cells in the leaf also have tiny pieces of a green substance called **CHLOROPHYLL**. This is why a leaf is green. The chlorophyll traps some of the sunlight and uses it to turn air, water and dissolved minerals into food.

Pores in the leaf

There are holes, or **LEAF PORES**, on the underside of the leaf. Around each leaf pore are two special cells called guard cells. When the leaf takes in or sends out air and water, the guard cells bend like bananas and the pores open. At all other times, the guard cells are straight and the leaf pores stay firmly closed (picture ②).

The pores open mainly in the day and are closed at night.

▼▶ ② **These two diagrams show how leaf pores work.**

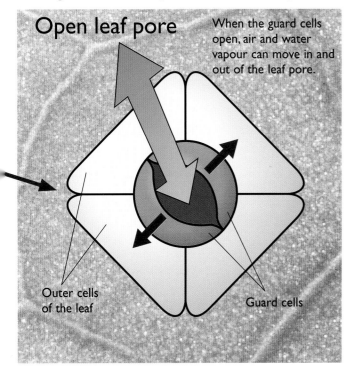

Open leaf pore

When the guard cells open, air and water vapour can move in and out of the leaf pore.

Outer cells of the leaf

Guard cells

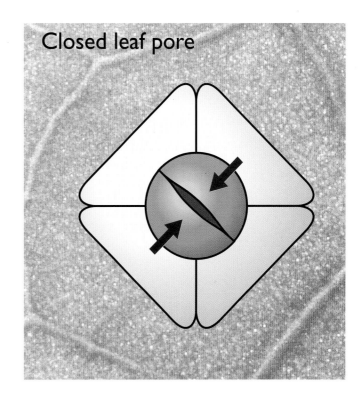

Closed leaf pore

How leaves make new tissue

Each part of a plant – leaves, stems, roots and flowers – is made from TISSUES. The cells that make the tissues are produced from sunlight, air, water and dissolved minerals.

Leaves make all the food they need from air, water and minerals in the soil. Sunlight provides the energy used to combine these materials into new cells. This process is called PHOTOSYNTHESIS (photo means light; synthesis means building). Here is how it works (picture ①).

SUNLIGHT

WATER and MINERALS

from the roots

Water and minerals travel up the roots through the water tubes in the stem, leaf stalk and veins.

+ CARBON DIOXIDE

from the surrounding air

All plants contain an element called CARBON. Carbon is found as a gas called CARBON DIOXIDE; which is part of the air.

...using energy from sunlight to produce...

ENERGY is trapped by chlorophyll in the cells of the leaf.

▲ ① Photosynthesis is the name of the process plants use to make new cells and tissues, and to get energy for living. It is a vital process for them and for us – we need the oxygen they send out during photosynthesis.

Storing food and energy

Plant leaves make food, which is stored in the roots, stems and **FRUIT** of the plant. This food is called **STARCH**. The stored starch is used as a source of energy at the end of the growing season, when the leaves die back (picture ②) and there is little sunlight.

▶ ② In winter, there is not enough sunlight for photosynthesis to take place. The green parts of many DECIDUOUS plants die back. The chlorophyll in the leaves of trees disappears and they turn different colours – brown, orange, red, etc. The trees then use the food they stored during the spring and summer.

OXYGEN

which is released into the surrounding air

Air contains **OXYGEN**, which the plant does not need. It is released through the leaf pores.

TISSUES

which the plant needs to grow

Flowers

Flowers develop from BUDS on the stem. They are designed to attract insects, birds and bats and so are often colourful or scented.

A **FLOWER** is the part of a **FLOWERING PLANT** that produces **SEEDS**.

From bud to flower

A flower forms inside a bud (picture ①). The outside of the bud is made from small, often green leaves. These protect the delicate parts of the flower while it is forming inside the bud.

When the flower is fully formed, the tiny leaves covering the bud move apart and the flower grows out between them.

Petals

PETALS are often the most noticeable part of a flower (picture ②). They are delicate sheets of **TISSUE** whose life is usually very short.

The number and shape of the petals can vary between different types of plant (picture ③). Many flowers have just four or five petals, but some have over twenty.

▼ ① The flowers on this stalk are emerging from their buds. The ones on the right are fully open.

Inside the flower

Flowers need to have both male and female parts if they are to make new seeds. The female parts form on a longer stalk in the centre of the flower, while the male parts usually form a ring of smaller stalks covered with a yellow powder called **POLLEN**.

▼▶ ② Inside the petals are small stalks. These are the male parts of the flower that make and release grains of pollen. The yellow pollen can be seen in this picture of a lily on the right. The larger stalk is the female part of the flower.

Petal

Female part of the flower.

Male part of the flower.

Yellow pollen produced by the male part of the flower.

The seed develops in the female part of the plant.

The leaves that covered the bud.

Stalk

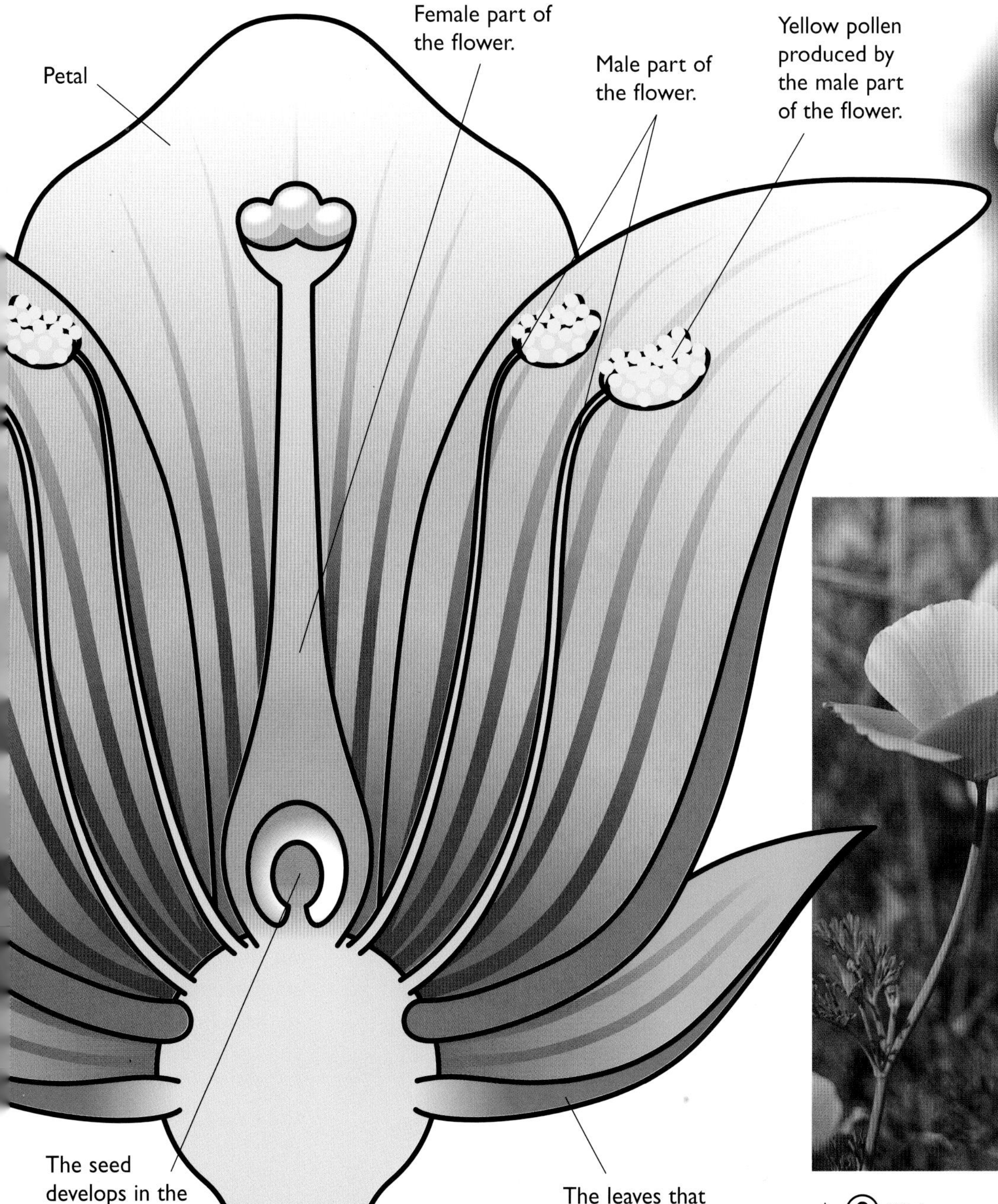

▲ ③ This poppy has sheet-like petals that spread wide apart.

How flowers share pollen

Plants make pollen so that they can produce new offspring. Before the offspring can be formed, the pollen must move from one plant to another in a process called POLLINATION.

Although a flower contains both male and female parts, most flowers cannot make seeds by themselves – they must find a way of carrying the male parts of one flower to the female parts of another flower.

The messenger for this is called pollen. After the female part of a flower has received pollen from the male parts of another flower, it can produce seeds.

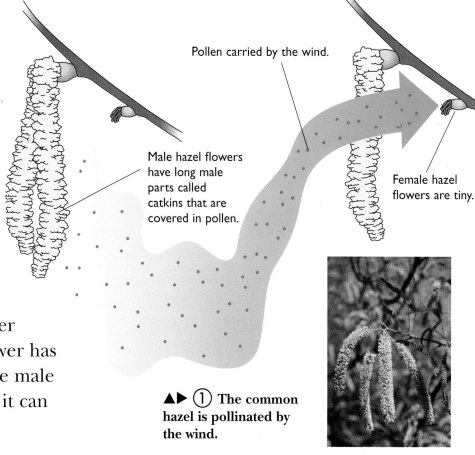

Pollen carried by the wind.

Male hazel flowers have long male parts called catkins that are covered in pollen.

Female hazel flowers are tiny.

▲▶ ① The common hazel is pollinated by the wind.

Sharing pollen

There are two main ways in which pollen can be shared: it can be carried on the wind, and it can be carried by insects and animals. Wind pollination is very common (as hay fever sufferers will know all too well, because their problem is caused by wind-carried pollen grains).

◀ ② While insects look for food they carry pollen from flower to flower. As they dip into a flower for its sugary nectar they pick up pollen on their bodies. Some of this pollen may be brushed off on to the female part of the next flower they visit. The bee (left) is covered in pollen and may visit hundreds of flowers in just one day.

Wind pollinated flowers

You may not have noticed wind pollinated flowers because they do not have colourful, scented petals. They simply release their pollen into the air and let the wind carry it to neighbouring plants (picture ①).

Insect pollinated flowers

Flowers that are pollinated by **INSECTS** often have brightly coloured flowers, and/or a strong scent, and they make a sugar substance called **NECTAR** (picture ②). The colour, and/or the scent, attracts the insects which land on the flower and begin to search for the sugary nectar that forms deep inside the flower. As the insect moves about inside the flower, pollen brushes onto it, and at the same time pollen from other plants are brushed onto the female part of the flower (picture ③).

▼ ③ Insect pollination happens when insects brush the pollen from one plant on to the female parts of the next plant they visit.

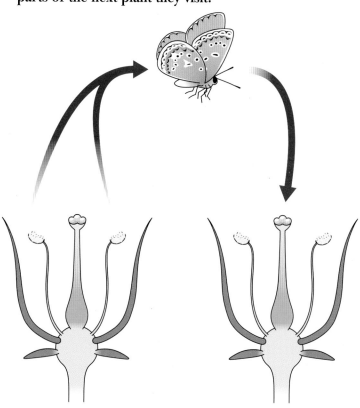

Seeds form

When the (male) pollen grain reaches a female part of a new plant, they combine and **SEEDS** begin to form at the base of the flower (picture ④). The base of the flower then swells, sometimes growing very large and developing into a **FRUIT** (picture ⑤).

▼ ④ After pollination, FERTILISATION occurs, and seeds begin to swell at the bottom of the flower, and the petals wither.

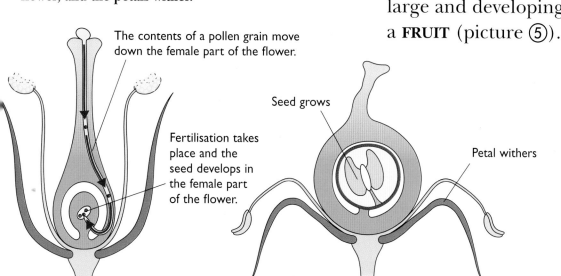

The contents of a pollen grain move down the female part of the flower.

Fertilisation takes place and the seed develops in the female part of the flower.

Seed grows

Petal withers

▲ ⑤ Here you can see the seed inside the fruit. This is an apricot.

Seeds and spores from non-flowering plants

Not all seed-making plants have flowers. Some plants produce seeds on cones, and still others produce SPORES.

Only some plants use flowers to make seeds. Many plants – including some that were on Earth long before the flowering plants – produce seeds in quite different ways.

Conifers

CONIFERS are common forest trees. They produce seeds in a woody, scaly case called a CONE (picture ①). There are two types of cone – male and female. The small male cone produces pollen which it releases into the air. The larger female cone forms seeds after it has received pollen from a male cone (picture ②).

▲ ① Conifer cones

▼ ② The life cycle of a conifer.

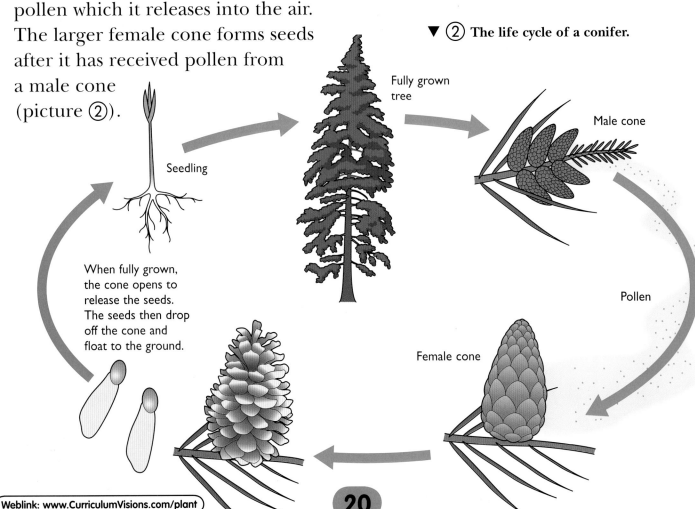

Fully grown tree

Seedling

Male cone

Pollen

Female cone

When fully grown, the cone opens to release the seeds. The seeds then drop off the cone and float to the ground.

Spores

A spore is a tiny bag which contains a piece of the parent plant. It is so small that you need a microscope to see a spore clearly. The spore floats through the air until it finds warm, moist conditions, then it breaks open and the piece of the parent plant grows up to form a new plant.

The green plants which produce spores include mosses and ferns (picture ③). Mushrooms and other FUNGI also produce spores.

Brown, button-shaped spore cases grow on the underside of fern leaves (picture ④). Spores are released from these cases.

Many fungi, like the mushroom, release spores from the underside of their cap (picture ⑤).

▲ ③ Moss with spore-producing stems. Spores are easily carried by the wind to land on soil far from the parent plant.

▲ ④ The brown, button-shaped spore cases on a fern or bracken are seen in this picture.

◄ ⑤ The underside of a mushroom cap opens to release spores.

21

How seeds are scattered

Plants have many ways of spreading their seeds. They may use the wind, animals or even water.

If seeds were not scattered, they would fall to the ground around the parent plant. Then, when the seeds began to grow, the **SEEDLING** roots would compete with each other, and the roots of the parent plant, for water and minerals. The leaves of the seedlings would overlap with each other and also would be shaded by the parent plant. They would not receive enough light to make all the food the plants need. The plants would not grow well.

However, when the seeds are spread out, the seedlings that grow

▶ ② These red, attractive fruits belong to a mountain ash. Birds eat them greedily for the nourishment in the fleshy outer part.

from them do not compete with each other and therefore have a better chance of growing into healthy plants.

Carried by the wind

Seeds can be scattered in many ways. The smallest seeds are so light that they can be carried by the wind.

Some small seeds, like dandelion, have a **PARACHUTE** of hairs to support them (picture ①). The parachute is carried by the wind, and the seed is blown a great distance from the parent plant.

◀ ① The dandelion is the most common example of how some small seeds use a parachute of hairs to support them.

Larger seeds, like the sycamore, have a type of wing. This allows the wind to blow them away from the parent plant as they fall from the tree.

Carried by animals

Soft, fleshy fruit often forms around large seeds (picture ②). These are then eaten by animals. The seeds are not **DIGESTED**, but pass through the animal whole, to be deposited elsewhere, surrounded by a ready-made pile of nutritious **MANURE**.

Some fruits have a spiky surface which can stick to fur or feathers (picture ③). These seeds, called **BURRS**, stick to passing animals or birds and may be carried many kilometres from the parent plant before they fall to the ground.

Carried by water

Some seeds can float or remain suspended in water without rotting. Such seeds can be carried thousands of kilometres before they float ashore. The coconut is a common example (picture ④).

▲ ③ This seed case has a large number of hooked spikes sticking out from it. These catch onto the fur of animals and provide an effective way of scattering the seed.

▼ ④ The coconut tree produces a very large seed. But it is lighter than water and able to float to another beach.

— The seeds of this coconut tree will drop into the water.

This beached coconut seed produces a seedling.

23

How seeds sprout

A seed contains both a tiny plant and a store of food. When conditions are favourable, the seed bursts open and the plant grows out.

Most seeds do not contain very much water: they are almost dry. There is just enough water left in the seed to keep the tiny plant alive, but there is not enough water present for the plant to grow.

The dry conditions inside the seed protect the plant and its food store in two ways. The dryness protects them from cold temperatures. If a water-filled seed was frozen, the water would expand as it turned into ice and would destroy the plant. The dry conditions also keep fungi from growing inside the seed and feeding on the plant and its store of food.

Germination

A seed does not sprout as soon as it leaves the parent plant. It remains inactive, or **DORMANT**, for some time.

Plants usually produce seeds at the end of the growing season. The weather conditions that follow the growing season are harsher, and if the seeds were to sprout, the tiny, new plant would not survive. The resting, or dormant, stage protects

Shoot

Tap root

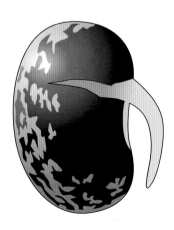

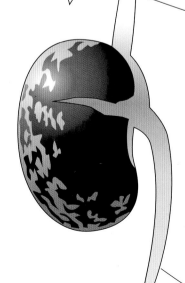

▲ ① A runner bean begins to germinate.

the seedling from growing in unfavourable conditions. When the next growing season occurs, the seed begins to grow. This early stage of growth is called **GERMINATION**.

Stages in germinating

The seed needs water and oxygen if it is to grow. At first, it begins to take these in through a small hole in the seed coat (picture ①).

The food stored in the seed is used by the tiny plant to give it the energy and materials to start growing.

As the plant grows it needs more water, so the first part of the plant to grow out of the seed is the root. When this happens we say that the seed has germinated.

Soon, the plant grows large enough to split open the seed coat. This allows more oxygen to reach the plant. Eventually the shoot emerges from the seed.

The shoot then grows rapidly upwards and the first pair of leaves unfurl (picture ②). With the leaves unfurled, the plant can now begin to make food and no longer has to rely on the food in its seed.

◀▼ ② **The development of the first leaves from a chestnut.**

weblink: www.CurriculumVisions.com/plant

Stems that produce new plants

Not all plants use seeds or spores to produce new plants. As some plants grow, they send out shoots from their stems and new plants develop from these.

It is possible for many plants to reproduce without creating seeds or spores at all. There are many ways that this happens, and some are shown below.

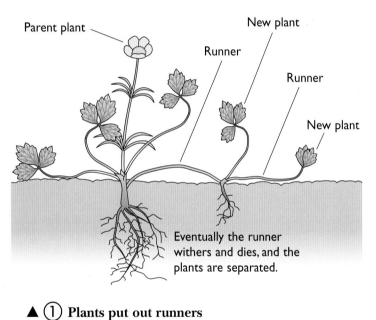

Parent plant

New plant

Runner

Runner

New plant

Eventually the runner withers and dies, and the plants are separated.

▲ ① **Plants put out runners that find their way into open spaces, and along which new plants grow and root. This picture shows a buttercup.**

▼ ② **These are the underground stems of an iris. The iris stores a large amount of food in its swollen stem.**

Runners

Some plants have side buds on their roots that grow long, thin, side shoots called **RUNNERS**. New buds then grow at intervals along the runner (picture ①).

In some cases, when a bud on a runner reaches the ground, it sprouts leaves and roots and forms a small copy of its parent.

In other cases, small plants form on runners before they reach the ground.

Underground stems

Another way that plants can grow is by sending stems horizontally through the soil. These plants send leaves and flower stalks into the air from joints on the underground stem (picture ②).

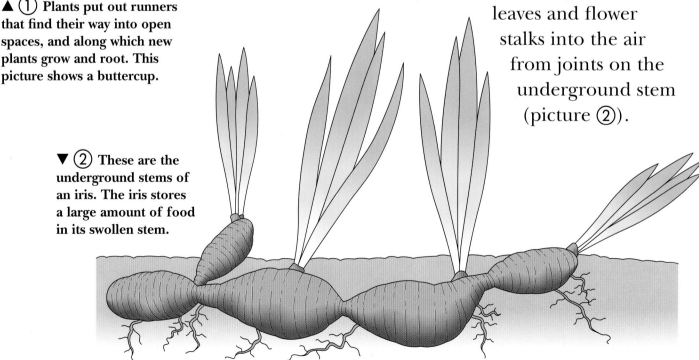

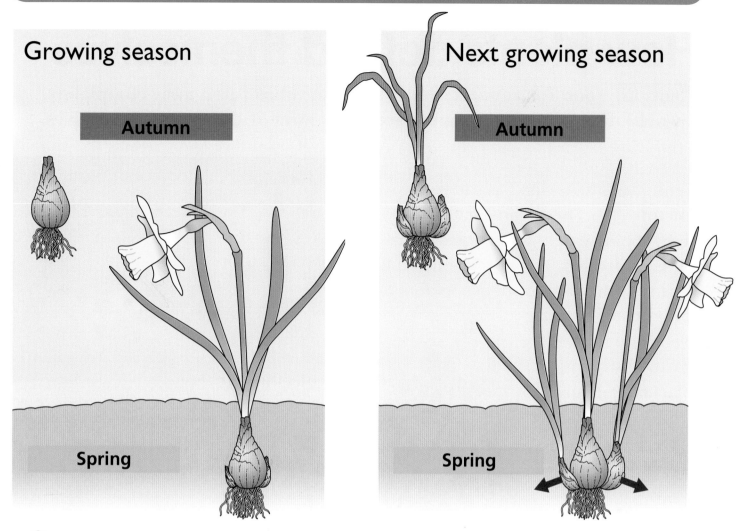

Growing season

Autumn

Spring

Next growing season

Autumn

Spring

▲ ③ Bulbs grow into plants, such as this daffodil, and are also able to grow side bulbs, which separate from the parent plant by the next growing season and form new plants.

Food is stored all along the underground stem. If the stem gets broken, each piece uses this food supply to form new, identical plants. This stem is called a **TUBER**.

Bulbs

A **BULB** is composed of a short stem surrounded by leaves. The bud contains a central bud and extra, side buds between the leaves.

While the central bud develops into the main plant, these side buds grow into tiny bulbs which later separate from the parent plant

(picture ③). Daffodils, tulips and hyacinths grow from bulbs.

Corms

A **CORM** is made from a short, thick stem that is swollen with food. The bud at the top of the corm produces the main shoot.

Side buds on the corm also produce shoots, and these make new corms. In time, these new corms separate from the old one and develop into separate (but identical) plants. Crocuses and gladioli produce corms.

Weblink: www.CurriculumVisions.com/plant

How plants defend themselves

Plants are food for animals. But if the plant were eaten away completely, it would die. As a result, plants have many ways of defending themselves.

Plants are food for animals as large as elephants and as small as caterpillars (picture ①). This means that plants are always being eaten. Sometimes plants are also affected by fire or damaged by storms. If they are to survive, plants must find ways of growing even though they are constantly being attacked (picture ②).

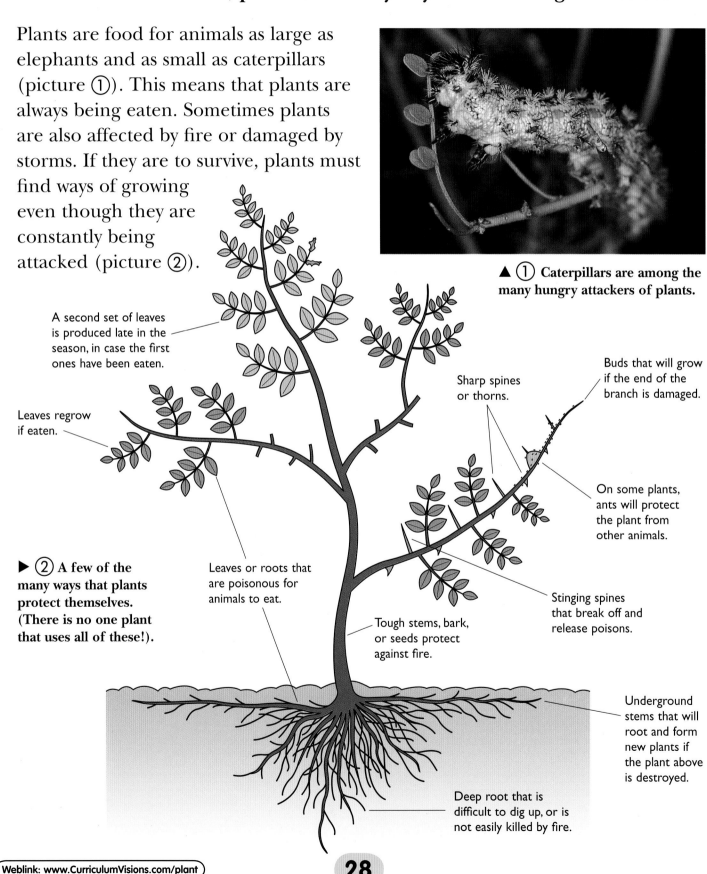

▲ ① Caterpillars are among the many hungry attackers of plants.

A second set of leaves is produced late in the season, in case the first ones have been eaten.

Leaves regrow if eaten.

Sharp spines or thorns.

Buds that will grow if the end of the branch is damaged.

On some plants, ants will protect the plant from other animals.

▶ ② A few of the many ways that plants protect themselves. (There is no one plant that uses all of these!).

Leaves or roots that are poisonous for animals to eat.

Stinging spines that break off and release poisons.

Tough stems, bark, or seeds protect against fire.

Underground stems that will root and form new plants if the plant above is destroyed.

Deep root that is difficult to dig up, or is not easily killed by fire.

How plants protect themselves

The grass in a meadow is eaten time after time, yet it still grows back. This is because grass defends itself by constantly growing new leaves from underground. Each new leaf is formed underground, well protected from the teeth of animals.

Spines and thorns

Not all plants continually replace their leaves in the same way as grass. Instead, they find ways of keeping animals at bay. Many grow THORNS (picture ③) and SPINES.

Poisons

Some plants, such as deadly nightshade and bracken, have POISONS in their leaves and are avoided by hungry animals. Other plants have hollow spines filled with poison, so that when an animal or person brushes

▶ ③ Plants such as roses use strong thorns as a defence.

against them, they snap off and the poison drips onto the skin causing a stinging sensation (picture ④).

Animal helpers

Some plants are helped by animals, especially ants. A swarm of ants can keep more or less any attacker at bay, no matter what its size. For this service, the plants provide a reward, for example a sugary sap, which the ants enjoy.

▼ ④ Nettles have poisonous spines.

29

How annuals compete

Once a plant has begun to sprout, it finds itself growing among many other plants, all competing for the same light, water and nourishment. Some plants, called annuals, grow quickly in order to out-compete their neighbours.

Plants do not live alone, but are surrounded by other living things. Each plant has to try to survive in among all of the others. To do this they have adapted to their surroundings in many ways.

Annuals

One way to survive is to grow faster than other plants nearby. This is what ANNUAL plants do. These are plants that grow, produce flowers and set seed all within a few weeks, often germinating in late spring or at the start of summer (picture ①).

▶ ① An annual plant will grow quickly even on open, sun-baked ground. This diagram shows the LIFE CYCLE of an annual.

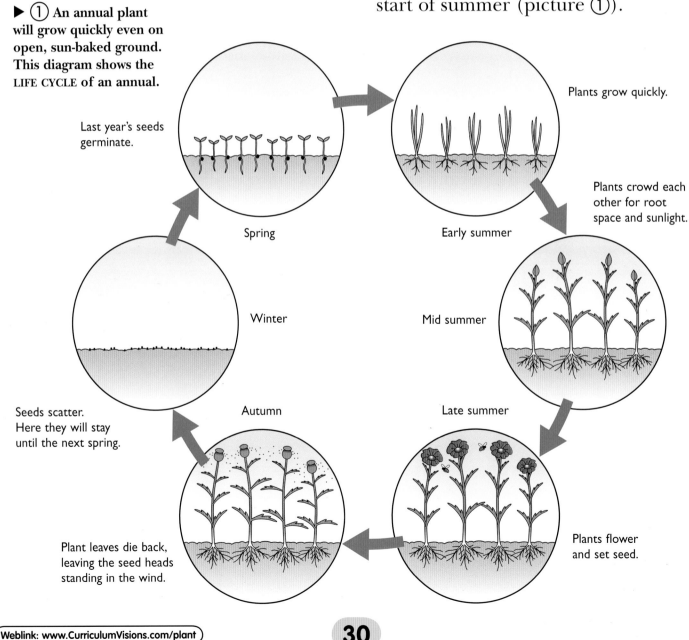

Last year's seeds germinate.

Spring

Plants grow quickly.

Early summer

Plants crowd each other for root space and sunlight.

Winter

Mid summer

Seeds scatter. Here they will stay until the next spring.

Autumn

Late summer

Plant leaves die back, leaving the seed heads standing in the wind.

Plants flower and set seed.

Annuals take over quickly

Plants with such short life cycles can spread to, or **COLONISE**, an area of bare ground quickly. Annual plants often have small seeds that are easily carried by the wind (picture ②). This is why they can still grow in fields that are cultivated each year (picture ③). Most of the '**WEEDS**' in a garden flower bed are annuals. A sign of their success is

how often people have to 'weed' their gardens (picture ④).

Annuals spend the period of harsh winter weather conditions as seeds. This saves the adult plant from having to develop ways of withstanding a cold or dry season.

▶ ② The stages of the poppy, a well-known annual plant. From left to right: bud; open flower with pollen; pollinated flower dying back; seed pod developed at bottom of flower (in cross-section and front view).

◀ ③ Poppies are such vigorously growing annual plants that they even grow in a field of wheat.

▶ ④ Many annual plants in a garden are called weeds.

How shrubs and trees compete

In general, the bigger the plant will become, the more slowly it grows. All shrubs and trees grow slowly, but eventually they shade out the faster-growing flowers and take over.

A plant that lives for many years is called a **PERENNIAL.** The larger perennials are called **SHRUBS**, and the largest of all are **TREES**. Their trunks make wood, which does not die back each year. The trunk is protected by an outer layer of bark.

How trees compete

Seeds from plants like trees cannot grow on open ground. They need moist soil, and they find this in shady places, such as beneath annual plants (picture ①).

Each year, they grow a bit more, until they grow above the annuals.

You can see how this takes place by imagining what might happen if a piece of ground is cleared of all trees and shrubs.

It does not take long before new plants are growing on the cleared land. These are mostly annual plants which have grown from seeds blown in on the wind.

At first, the annual plants may cover the ground (see page 30).

▼ ① The way that trees compete is by growing taller than all other plants. This diagram shows a long period of time. It would take tens of years for the trees to grow up fully.

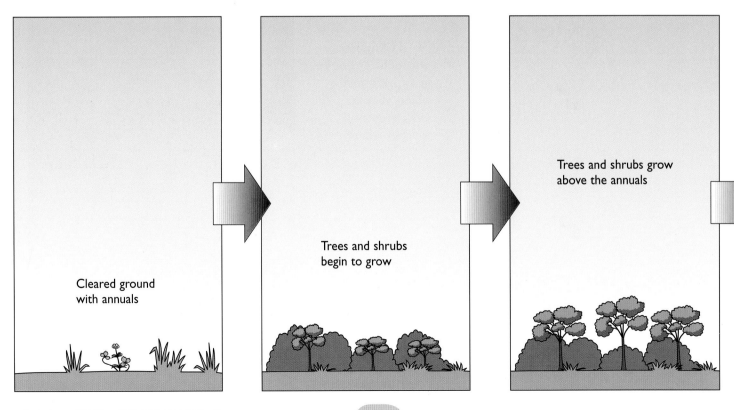

Cleared ground with annuals

Trees and shrubs begin to grow

Trees and shrubs grow above the annuals

But, within a year or two, other plants may begin to grow and make it too shady for the annual seeds to germinate.

In time, the quick-flowering (annual) plants are replaced by (perennial) shrubs and trees. The most successful of these are trees, because they grow above all of the other plants, shading them out (picture ②). This is why most areas of **WILDERNESS** are forests.

Once trees have taken over, things do not change. As each tree dies, it is replaced by another. But if the land is cleared again, for example, by a fire, then this gives annuals the chance to grow once more.

◀ ② **Here you can see a woodland that is still developing. The trees have not yet completely shaded the ground.**

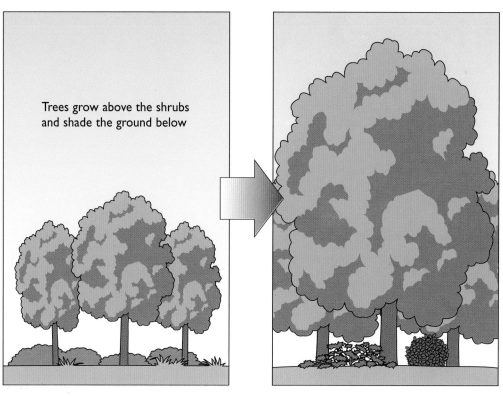

Trees grow above the shrubs and shade the ground below

Trees are now fully grown and the ground is too shady for most other plants to compete. The plants that live below the trees grow up and flower early in the year, before the trees come in to leaf.

Habitats

Plants grow almost everywhere in the world. To survive, they have to be adapted in many ways.

Plants live together in places like forests, deserts, meadows and so on. Each plant lives where it is best suited. The different kinds of homes are called **HABITATS**.

The weather is not the same across the world. In some places there is little water, others have freezing winters or scorching summers.

No plant can live in all of these conditions, which is why you find different plants across the world (picture ①). Here are some of the main habitats in the world.

The tundra

The tundra is the name given to parts of the world close to the ice-cold poles. Here, the summers are too short and the winters too long and harsh for trees to grow.

The plants that are best adapted to long winters and blizzards are those which keep close to the ground and have thick, waxy leaves. There is little sunlight so they grow very slowly. These kinds of plants are often known as **ALPINES**.

▼ ① **The pattern of plants across the world.**

Coniferous forest: very cold in winter, with frozen ground. Very short summer.

Woodland: warm in summer and cold in winter, but moist all year.

Tundra: too cold for trees

Prairies: natural grasslands, too dry for trees.

Arctic or Antarctic

The coniferous forests

Conifers are best adapted to long winters and a short growing season. They have tough, needle-shaped leaves. By keeping their leaves all year, they do not have to find enough energy to grow new ones each year. A spruce tree is a typical tree of the **CONIFEROUS FOREST**.

Woodland

WOODLANDS grow in warmer areas than conifers. Woodland trees grow broad leaves so they can soak up the sun's energy quickly in summer. An oak is a typical woodland plant.

Deserts

Deserts occur where there is little rainfall, and what rain there is falls very unreliably. Plants that survive in a desert either have very deep tap roots, or they store water in their stems. Cacti are typical desert plants.

Tropical rainforests

RAINFORESTS contain some of the world's biggest plants. With lots of sunshine, hot air and rain almost every day, these plants can soar into the sky.

Rainforest trees are adapted to get the sunlight they need by having tall straight trunks with no side branches.

Desert: too dry even for most grasses.

Savanna: hot and dry for much of the year. Grasses with some trees.

Rainforest: hot and wet all year. Trees grow well.

Equator

Woodland through the seasons

A woodland changes dramatically through the seasons. The lives of both plants and animals are adapted to the changes.

Trees that grow in cool climates with a cold winter shed their leaves in autumn. These are called **DECIDUOUS** trees. When they grow together, they make a **WOODLAND**. Here you can see how the woodland changes through the seasons.

The canopy

The trees grow until their branches fit together to make a covering of leaves called a **CANOPY** (picture ①).

This is how the leaves get the light they need from the sun. The canopy is thick with leaves for part of the year, but in winter, the leaves are gone and the branches bare, windswept and cold.

The woodland floor

Many plants and animals live below the canopy. Buds, leaves, flowers, and falling fruit and nuts all provide food for animals that live on the woodland floor.

▼ ① The way that woodland plants change through the seasons.

Winter

Most woodland plants are deciduous and stand leafless during the winter.

Animals, such as jays and squirrels, eat the acorns they have buried during the Autumn.

Evergreen shrubs, such as holly, keep their leaves.

Snowdrops are the first plants to flower at the end of winter.

Leaves begin to **DECAY** and rot. They will gradually release nourishment back to the soil.

Spring

At the end of spring, leaves start to sprout on trees.

Primroses and other small woodland floor plants flower.

Bluebells begin to flower at the end of spring.

Adapting to the seasons

Because the amount of light in the woodland changes so much with the seasons, the plants that live in the woodland have adapted to it.

Every plant needs light. In the height of summer the trees shade the ground, which means that the other plants have to be adapted to grow early, before the trees come into leaf, or to live in the shade.

Growing early

Some plants begin to grow in winter. Snowdrops are the first to shoot, even flowering while snow may still be on the ground. As the months pass, they are followed by primroses and then bluebells.

All of these plants use the food they have stored from the previous year. They do not need the ground to warm up, or the sun to shine strongly, to begin their annual growth. By late spring they have flowered and set seed almost before the other plants have even started putting on leaves.

Summer shade

Plants that grow on the woodland floor in summer have to be adapted to live in a partly shady place. They have broad leaves that can soak up even small amounts of light. But this is not an easy place to grow, so the woodland floor is not thickly covered by plants in summer.

Summer

Trees spread their leaves to get as much sunlight as possible.

Ferns, mosses and fungi grow in the shade of the trees.

Autumn

Trees take back food stored in the leaves. Leaves turn brown and fall off.

Holly produces berries which are eaten by animals during the winter.

Jays and squirrels store nuts in ground.

Leaves begin to build up on the forest floor.

How plants are adapted to water

A pond is a special kind of environment, or habitat, in which many plants live. Different types of plants share a pond by choosing different places to live.

All of the plants in a pond need a supply of light and nourishment. The nourishment comes from the water, so the main concern of the plants is to gather enough light. To do this, some may have leaves that stand out of the water, while others have leaves that float on the surface of the water (picture ①). Some plants can make do with smaller amounts of light. These have their leaves beneath the surface. In this way, a complicated **COMMUNITY** of plants can all grow in the same pond, each making different uses of the environment.

▼ ① **The different types of plants in a pond.**

Reeds and rushes are examples of pond-edge plants. Their roots are adapted to take in oxygen from the water. Their deep roots help them to survive periods in summer when water levels fall and the pond edge becomes dry land.

Water lilies have long-stemmed plate-shaped, floating leaves and supple stems.

Floating plants have short roots to provide balance.

Pond weeds that live below the surface tend to have ribbon or fernlike leaves because this gives them a large surface to absorb light.

Algae do not need a stem because they are supported by the water. When they occur in great numbers, they make the water turn a green colour.

Fish eat the plants which keeps them from overcrowding. The waste from the fish provides nourishment for other plants.

How water plants adapt

The waterlogged mud of the pond bottom does not contain enough oxygen for the roots to thrive, and so water plants have developed spaces inside their stems that can feed air down to the roots.

Most plants that live in ponds are perennials. Their shoots die back at the end of the growing season, but their roots remain alive. This is why a pond in winter looks very different from in summer.

In a pond, you might expect to find the following kinds of plants:

Floating plants

Some plants float on the surface like small boats. They have a short root that dangles into the water. The root acts like a weight on the bottom of a fishing float, helping to keep the rest of the plant upright. These plants can survive even in deep water.

Submerged plants

Some plants remain under water throughout their lives, relying on the water for support (picture ②).

Most are small plants which need only small roots to hold them in place. These plants take in water, carbon dioxide and minerals through their leaves, and use their roots only as an anchor.

Plants with floating leaves

Some plants have roots in the mud at the bottom of the pond, but long stalked leaves that float on the surface. However, there is a limit to the depth of water that these plants can grow in, and so they are only found around the edges of the pond.

Plants that stand clear of the water

In the shallow water around the edges of the pond, plants can anchor themselves in the boggy mud and then grow up through the water and out into the air. These plants often have tall stems and need strong roots to hold them upright.

▶ ② Like other plants, pond weeds give out oxygen when they are in sunlight. The brighter the sunshine, the more oxygen they produce. You can see the bubbles of oxygen being given out by the leaves of this plant.

Mountain plants

Many mountain plants have to survive through cold, wind and snow. Only the hardiest and best adapted plants can survive these harsh conditions.

All mountain plants have to be tough. However, the lower slopes are more sheltered and this is where forests can grow. Higher up the mountain, conditions are too severe for trees, and the upper slopes are home only to meadow and alpine plants (pictures ① and ②).

The forest zone

The lowest slopes of a mountain may be warm enough for broadleaved trees to grow. But these trees need warm summers and are not found further up the slopes of a mountain. Instead, the higher slopes are covered with conifers, which have small, waxy needles instead of broad leaves (picture ③).

Near the top of the forest zone, conditions are too harsh even for conifers to grow well, and trees become more stunted.

The treeless zone

Above the forest, some grasses will grow, but higher than this only small, woody alpine plants can survive (picture ④). The alpines hug the ground, or shelter between boulders. They are perennials, with a life-span of many years. Few annual plants grow here – it takes many years of slow, determined growth for a plant just to get big enough to flower.

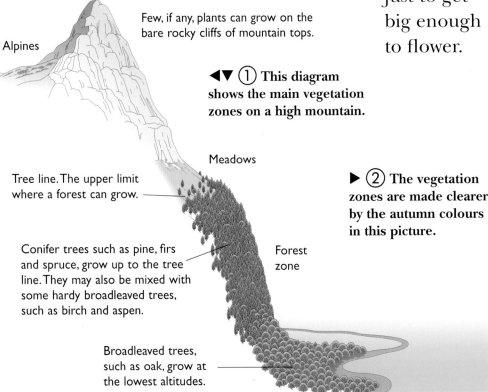

Few, if any, plants can grow on the bare rocky cliffs of mountain tops.

Alpines

◄▼ ① This diagram shows the main vegetation zones on a high mountain.

Meadows

Tree line. The upper limit where a forest can grow.

Conifer trees such as pine, firs and spruce, grow up to the tree line. They may also be mixed with some hardy broadleaved trees, such as birch and aspen.

Forest zone

Broadleaved trees, such as oak, grow at the lowest altitudes.

▶ ② The vegetation zones are made clearer by the autumn colours in this picture.

▼ ③ **The many adaptations shown by plants in the forest zone.**

Conifers have shallow roots that spread out to capture as much nourishment as possible from the thin soils. Conifers can also survive long winters when the ground is frozen hard and no water can reach the roots.

Just above the tree line, summer meadows contain grasses and flowers such as wild lupins (below) and buttercups. These bloom after the spring snowmelt.

Conifers are well adapted for long, cold winters and deep snowfalls. They have fine, downward-sloping needle-shaped leaves that readily shed the snow. The needles stay on from year-to-year because the growing season is too short for leaves to regrow each spring. The needles are dark-coloured to soak up as much heat as possible.

Bilberry and mosses grow on the poor dark soils under the conifers.

▼▶ ④ **The many adaptations shown by plants high in the treeless zone.**

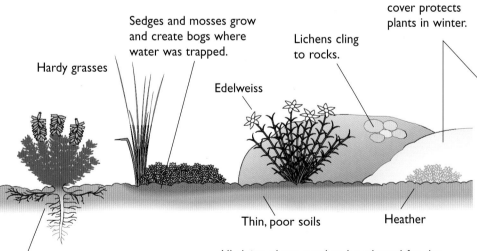

Hardy grasses

Sedges and mosses grow and create bogs where water was trapped.

Edelweiss

Lichens cling to rocks.

Insulating snow cover protects plants in winter.

Thin, poor soils

Heather

Alpines need to store as much heat as possible. Many are tufted, have furry leaves and grow in dense, low bushes. Many even make their own antifreeze. The leaves are dark green to soak up as much of the sun's heat as possible.

All alpine plants need to be adapted for dry conditions. This may seem strange, when they may be covered in snow for half the year. But the water in snow is locked up as ice and so plants cannot use it. Then, as soon as the snow melts, harsh winds dry out the ground. To cope with this, even plants that seem tiny when seen on the surface may have deep tap roots that seek for water far underground.

Alpines have to make good use of the short growing season. As soon as the snow melts, they shoot, flower and set seed – giving the spectacular blossoms for which mountains are so famous. The entire growing season may last only three months.

Adapting in the tropical rainforest

The year-round heat, strong sunlight and high amount of moisture found in many places close to the equator means that these places are filled with plants. This causes intense competition.

Imagine a world where it is hot all year round, where rain falls nearly every day and where the sun rises high in the sky. This is the **TROPICAL RAINFOREST**. Here are found all of the conditions needed for rapid growth (picture ①).

There are no seasons in a tropical rainforest, so there is no season when the plants need to shed their leaves. Therefore, nearly all rainforest plants are **EVERGREENS**.

▲ ① Tropical rainforests are made of tall trees with few low branches. They look like giant natural umbrellas. Some trees have trunks that spread out near the ground. These are often called BUTTRESS ROOTS because they look as though they grew like that to support the tall trunks.

Many plants set seed in the soil on the ground then grow long climbing stems which grip the trunk of a nearby tree for support. When the tip of the stem reaches the sunlight it produces leaves. The best known climbing plants in the rainforest are called lianas.

▲ ② The branches of the trees form homes for smaller plants such as mosses, ferns and orchids. Some of these plants have leaves which form a cup for collecting rain water.

Poor soil

The soils of rainforests are ancient. They have experienced millions of years of heavy rain. This has washed away all of the nourishment from the soil. As a result, all of the plants in a rainforest have to be masters of storing whatever nourishment they can get (picture ②).

Plants in a rainforest get their nourishment from two places: from the rain that falls, and from other plants that have died and are rotting on the forest floor.

Giant trees

Some of the world's biggest trees are found in rainforests (picture ③). But they have to work hard to get the nourishment they need. To do this, they send out roots just below the surface, so that, as the nourishment is washed away from the rotting plants, they can capture it and use it straight away.

The largest trees in a tropical rainforest have branches like the spokes of an open umbrella. They push their branches up to the sun and the leaves make an almost closed surface, or canopy. This canopy is very high, often about 30m from the ground.

◀ ③ A rainforest tree with buttress roots.

Deserts

Deserts are mainly hot places with very unreliable rainfall. Very few plants can survive such difficult conditions.

Deserts are places where little rain falls and there can be many months without any rain. Most deserts are hot and sunny, so desert plants have to be specially adapted to hold on to whatever moisture they can get (picture ①).

Plants with a short life

Plants are adapted to desert life in two ways. One group are annuals, whose seeds lie in the desert soil until rain comes. Then, they race to germinate, grow, flower and set seed – all before the ground dries out. This may all happen in a few weeks.

Plants that grow slowly

The other group of desert plants are perennials. During the long periods without rain, they simply stop growing. Then, just after a rainstorm, they grow leaves and burst into flower.

▼ ① **The ways in which desert plants are adapted to survive.**

Saguaro cactus

The cactus stores water in its stem.

To protect it against animals this cactus has spines, but they can only be seen close to – see the picture on page 45.

There are no leaves to reduce the amount of water lost to the hot dry desert air.

The saguaro cactus has a network of roots close to the surface to catch any rain that seeps into the soil.

Plants such as this creosote bush have very long tap roots to find water. As with many plants in the desert, they also have small, leathery leaves.

Some desert perennials have deep tap roots to find water even when it has seeped deep underground (picture ②). To prevent losing water, they have small, waxy leaves with few leaf pores (picture ③).

Others, such as the cactus, store water in fleshy stems than can swell with water. They have no leaves at all; their green stems make all the food they need (picture ④).

▼ ② This shrub (called a creosote bush because of the smell of its leaves) has only a tenth of the plant above ground. Below ground, there may be a huge tap root 15 m, or more, long. Notice that the plant has very small leaves.

▼ ③ Like the creosote bush, the leaves of the palo verde bush are tiny and fleshy to reduce water loss. The small leaves cannot produce much food and so this plant compensates by producing food from its stems. In extreme drought it can shed leaves and stems to reduce water loss.

◀ ④ This is a close-up of a saguaro cactus, one of the world's biggest cacti. They have shallow roots that spread out like a net just below the surface. They keep reserves of water in their swollen stems and protect themselves from attack with sharp spines.

Weblink: www.CurriculumVisions.com/plant

Glossary

ADAPT The way in which a plant is suited to where it grows. If something is well adapted to where it grows, it will be more likely to survive.

ALPINE The name given to a group of plants that can survive the harsh conditions of high mountains, where there is prolonged snowfall, frequent frost, stoney soils, high winds and intense sun.

ANNUAL A plant which completes its life cycle in a single growing season (but not necessarily a year).

BARK The outer layers of a woody stem. The inner bark is soft and contains the growing layer and the tubes that carry food and water from the roots to the leaves. The outer bark is harder and made mainly of corky, dead tissue. The cells of the outer bark protect the inner, growing bark from damage by storm, fire and many animals.

BLADE The thin, usually flat part that makes up the bulk of a leaf. The rest of the leaf is made up of the stalk. The blade is strengthened by a pattern of veins.

BROADLEAVED TREES The name for trees which have flat leaf blades. Some broadleaved trees are deciduous and shed their leaves seasonally, while others are evergreens. Most broadleaved trees would also be called hardwoods.

BUD A newly developing part of a plant stem which is often protected by young leaves. Some buds simply grow longer and make a plant taller or broader, while others develop into flowers. A flower bud contains young petals rather than young leaves.

BULB The resting stage of some flowering plants. It consists of a short stem which is surrounded by leaves. The stem is swollen with stored food from the last season's growth. When the correct conditions (such as the warmth of spring) stimulate the plant to start using the stored food, it grows rapidly, pushing out leaves and stalks from the top of the bulb. Lilies, hyacinths and onions are examples of plants with bulbs.

BURR The name for any kind of seed case that has hooks on it, and which will attach to any passing animal. Burrs are a common and very effective means of carrying seeds to new environments.

BUTTRESS ROOTS A special shape of root which leaves the stem (trunk) above ground. Buttress roots are often thin and plank-like. Buttress roots may help in supporting tall trees, and by sending roots out further from the stem, they may also be useful in reaching nourishment from a wider area. Almost all buttress roots grow on tropical trees.

CACTUS (CACTI) A group of woody-stemmed perennial plants which usually have spines and produce brightly coloured flowers. Cacti mostly grow in dry, desert conditions, and have leaves that are small or missing to stop them losing water. The green stem takes over the role of making food and energy from sunlight, a role that leaves would otherwise perform.

Many cacti cells are specially developed to store water. Roots of cacti are usually fibrous and shallow, forming a net of roots that allows them to gather any rain seeping into the ground.

CANOPY The covering of leaves that forms when tall trees grow close together.

CARBON A chemical element and one of the fundamental building blocks of life.

CARBON DIOXIDE A gas made of a combination of carbon and oxygen and which is found in small quantities in the air. Carbon dioxide is essential to plant growth.

CELL The tiny building blocks of all life. All but the simplest kinds of plants contain many kinds of cells, each specialised for a particular role.

CELLULOSE A material that forms the walls of plant cells and gives them support.

CHLOROPHYLL A green substance which can trap some of the energy in sunlight and use it to cause chemical changes that produce food from carbon dioxide gas.

COLONISE To spread to a new area, to move to a new place.

COMMUNITY A group of plants that live together with animals in an area of similar climate.

CONE The equivalent of a flower for conifers. It is a cone-shaped mass of papery scales. Coniferous trees have male cones, which carry pollen, and female cones, which develop seeds.

CONIFER Any plant that bears its seeds and pollen on separate cones.

Conifers belong to the plant group called gymnosperms, meaning that their seeds grow without the protection of a fruit (as is the case for flowering plants). Most conifers are evergreen trees with needle-shaped leaves.

CONIFEROUS FOREST A type of community where the largest number of trees are conifers.

CORM A short, fat, underground stem which is swollen with food. It is different from a bulb, which contains young leaves.

DECAY A process in which the tissues of dead plants and animals break down into simple substances that can be used as food by living things.

DECIDUOUS A type of woody plant which loses all its leaves at the end of each growing season. In cooler parts of the world, most deciduous plants lose their leaves as temperatures fall, or with the first frosts.

DIGESTED Broken down in the intestines of an animal into small particles which are absorbed by the animals blood.

DORMANT A state in a plant's life cycle when it does not show signs of activity such as growing or flowering.

ENERGY The ability to do work.

EVERGREEN A plant which stays in leaf all year round. As it loses some leaves it grows others so that its branches never look bare. Many broadleaved evergreens have leaf blades that are thicker and more leathery than those of deciduous trees and many, such as conifers, are needlelike.

FERTILISATION The process in which the male and female cells join together.

FIBRE A solid thread which grows inside a shoot or root and gives the plant support.

FIBROUS ROOT A thin root that may branch from a tap root or may be part of a mass of roots that branch from the base of the stem.

FLOWER The part of a flowering plant that contains the seed-producing part of the plant. The most obvious parts of a flower are the thin sheets of tissue called petals. Inside the petals are the male and female parts of a flower that will produce seeds.

FLOWERING PLANT A group of plants which produce flowers and fruits containing seeds.

FRUIT The swollen and fleshy part of a shoot that develops at the base of a flower. It contains the seeds. An apple is an example of a fruit.

FUNGI A plant-like living thing which produces spores and feeds on the decaying bodies of plants and animals. Mushrooms are examples of fungi.

GERMINATE/GERMINATION The process in which a seed takes in water and breaks open its seed coat to release the root.

HABITAT The place that a particular plant (or animal) is most suited to.

INSECT An animal with six legs, and usually, two pairs of wings.

LEAF PORES The openings, usually on the underside of the leaf, through which a plant takes in carbon dioxide from the air and sends out water vapour and oxygen. Also called stomata.

LEAF/LEAVES The flat, blade-shaped and normally green part of a plant that catches sunlight. Cells in a leaf use sunlight as energy to make food.

LIFE CYCLE The series of stages in the growth of a plant, from its development as a seed until it has reproduced and died.

MANURE A general name for the solid waste products from animals. It is rich in minerals for plant growth.

MINERAL A chemical which is necessary for life. A plant takes in minerals through its roots, dissolved in the water it sucks up from the soil.

NECTAR A sweet, sticky substance, produced by flowers, which attracts animals such as insects, bats and humming birds.

NEEDLE A long, narrow, rod-like leaf often found on conifer trees.

NUCLEUS The inside part of the cell which controls the growth, development and activities of the cell.

NUTRIENT A substance needed by an organism for healthy growth. Nutrients can be minerals or substances produced by plants or animals.

OXYGEN A chemical element released by plants during photosynthesis.

PARACHUTE A device which allows a heavy object like a seed to sink slowly enough through the air for it to be carried some distance from its parent plant.

PERENNIAL A plant which lives for many years.

PETAL A large, coloured blade in a flower. It acts like a flag, making sure that the flower is easily spotted by insects.

PHOTOSYNTHESIS The process in which the green chlorophyll in a plant uses the energy in sunlight to make food and oxygen from water and carbon dioxide.

POISON A substance that can cause harm to a living thing if it becomes absorbed.

POLLEN Yellow-coloured grains that are produced by the male parts of a flower.

POLLINATION The transfer of pollen between the male parts of one flower and the female parts of another flower.

RAINFOREST A community of plants that grows in an area where rainfall occurs throughout much of the year. In the areas near the equator, rainforests are called tropical rainforests.

ROOT The part of a plant that anchors it to the ground or some other support. A plant root is normally found underground. It takes in water and dissolved minerals from the soil so that they can pass up the stem to the leaves. Roots also store food (as seen clearly, for example, in a carrot).

RUNNER A side shoot from the main stem, which grows horizontally above the surface of the ground.

SEED A miniature plant, together with a supply of food protected by a hard coating. Seeds of flowering plants form at the base of a flower. As the seed matures, the base of the flower forms a swollen, rounded shape called a fruit.

SEEDLING A name for a plant between germination and when it becomes totally independent of the food stored in the seed.

SHOOT The stem of a plant that has just begun to grow from a seed.

SHRUB A woody plant with many stems and usually less than 3 metres tall.

SOIL A mixture of rock particles and the decaying remains of plants and animals which forms the top layer of the ground.

SPINE Sharply pointed part of a woody stem. Spines are one of the ways plants defend themselves from being eaten.

SPORE A structure which contains a piece of the parent which is capable of growing into a new plant.

STARCH A substance that plants use as stored food.

STALK On small plants, for example, annuals, the stalk is the term used for the main stem. Stalks also connect leaves and fruit to branches of larger plants.

STEM The main body, or stalk, of a plant that supports the flowers and leaves and allows food and water to be transported around the plant. Most stems are above ground but some stems, such as irises, form underground.

TAP ROOT A thick, central root that anchors the plant and helps the plant collect water.

THORN Sharply pointed curved part of a woody stem. Thorns are one of the ways plants defend themselves from being eaten.

TISSUE The material from which plants are made. Each kind of tissue is made of one kind of cell. New tissues are made at the tips of the shoots and roots.

TRANSPIRATION The loss of water through the tiny pores that are situated mainly on the underside of leaves.

TREE A perennial woody plant that has a single main trunk and grows more than 4 or 5 metres tall.

TREE RINGS The seasonal rings seen in a cross section of a tree trunk, due to its growth in a particular season of the year (for example, spring and summer).

TROPICAL The region around the equator between the Tropics of Cancer (23° 27' N) and Capricorn (23° 27' S).

TRUNK The large, woody stem of a tree.

TUBER A swelling on a shoot or root in which food is stored.

VEIN Long, thin supporting 'scaffolding' in a leaf that also carries water and food between the leaf and the stem. Veins are made from fibres and tubes.

WEED Any plant that has grown unwanted in a cultivated plot like a garden or farm field.

WILDERNESS A place in which the effects of people are still small.

WOODLAND The community which is home to deciduous trees like oak.

Weblink: www.CurriculumVisions.com/plant

Index